LISTEN
to the
BIRDS

Donald Kroodsma

Léna Mazilu

Yoann Guény

Norton Young Readers

An Imprint of W. W. Norton & Company
Celebrating a Century of Independent Publishing

For children of all ages, that they may appreciate the magic of birdsong.—D.K.

For my family—L.M.

For information about permission to reproduce selections from this book, write to
Permissions, W. W. Norton & Company, Inc., 500 Fifth Avenue, New York, NY 10110

For information about special discounts for bulk purchases, please contact
W. W. Norton Special Sales at specialsales@wwnorton.com or 800-233-4830

Manufacturing by RRD Asia
Book design by Hana Anouk Nakamura
Production manager: Delaney Adams

ISBN: 978-1-324-03103-1

W. W. Norton & Company, Inc.
500 Fifth Avenue, New York, N.Y. 10110
www.wwnorton.com

W. W. Norton & Company Ltd.
15 Carlisle Street, London W1D 3BS

1 2 3 4 5 6 7 8 9 0

AN INTRODUCTION TO BIRDSONG

Birds don't croak or growl or howl or bark. They sing, often with music so beautiful that we stop to smile at the magic. What fun, then, to learn who the magicians are.

It takes practice, but you can learn to identify these hidden singers by their voices. In this book we'll listen to thirty-five common birds: woodpeckers, doves, owls, and so many more. We'll take two walks, one in eastern North America and one in western North America, and discover some of the different birds that sing in these different regions—and some that sing in both.

Birds often sing from the treetops, as if saying "LISTEN TO ME!" It's almost always the male who is singing, to impress females and to defend his territory. Sometimes the songs are long, complicated melodies. Sometimes they are just a few notes.

He may be the one singing, but it is many generations of females who have decided what he should sing. You see, if a female bird doesn't like a male's song, he won't be the father of her children. The females decide who the good singers are, and only good singers have kids, who, if they are boys, will in turn sing like their fathers! You can think of the female songbird as the silent composer of the great birdsong orchestra that we hear.

Besides *songs*, all birds have *calls*. Usually, only the male sings, but both male and female birds use many simpler calls. One call might be used to warn of a hawk nearby, another to chase predators away from the nest.

Some birds, like owls or doves, have songs and calls that are *innate*—that means the birds have an instinct to make those sounds as soon as they're born (well, hatched). Then there's a special group of about five thousand species of small birds that learn their songs by listening to other birds, just like human babies learn to speak by copying the sounds other people make. You might hear a young bird, about two months old, babbling just like a human child as he practices the songs he's learning. These are known as *songbirds*, and they have more complex brains that enable them to learn like this.

This makes the songbirds especially fun to listen to. They often sing in *dialects*, with songs that sound different from one place to another. It's like a person speaking with an accent. Some songbirds, such as the mockingbird, can learn more than a hundred different songs, and can *mimic*, or copy, the songs of other species as well. They sometimes learn sounds of the human-made world, too, such as car alarms and cell phone ringers.

A bird's beautiful music comes from its voice box, or *syrinx*, the part of the throat that creates sound. If you put your hand on your throat and hum, you can feel the vibration of your vocal cords. Humans have only one voice box (called a *larynx*), but each songbird has two. A songbird can sing a duet all by himself!

Once you learn to recognize the songs, what's next? There's much more you can do to become an expert listener. But first, let's begin our walk.

HOW TO USE THIS BOOK
WITH A SMARTPHONE OR TABLET

A picture—and a song—are worth a thousand words! This book can be used with the free **birdie memory** mobile application: point a smartphone or tablet at the illustrations and watch the birds come alive and sing.

TO USE THE APPLICATION

1. Download and install the free **birdie memory** app by pointing your phone or tablet's camera at the QR code, or by visiting the iTunes or Google Play store.

2. Follow the tutorial and start listening and learning!

The **birdie memory** app has two modes:

OBSERVATION MODE
Point your device's camera to any of the birds illustrated in this book. The bird on your device will come alive and sing.

MEMORY MODE
Listen to a birdsong on your device, then point it to the illustrations to see if you can match it with the right bird.

EASTERN NORTH AMERICA

OUR DAWN WALK

We'll start very early, in the park on the edge of town. The birds sing their finest songs just before the sun comes up. So we'll meet before sunrise, under the streetlight by the park's visitor center. Set your alarm! Bring your binoculars, a water bottle, maybe a snack.

We'll follow the trail to the woods and back, through different habitats where a variety of birds live. The world will be all ours then—almost no one else is awake. But we'll be there, out in the early dawn, listening for the birds.

THE PARK ON THE EDGE OF TOWN

AMERICAN ROBIN

Cheerily, cheer-up, cheerio, cheerily eek

Here we are, right on time! Just beyond the streetlight, the world seems dark and quiet. But here by the light, a robin sings the morning's first song.

Just listen to him! It sounds like he's singing for joy. We can't know what he's thinking, but we can certainly feel happy listening to him.

He sings strong, clear notes, moving quickly from one to the next. Sing along with him and feel the rhythm: it sounds like he's saying *cheerily, cheer-up, cheerio, cheerily*. After a few of those low twitters, he screeches a much higher note. It sounds like he's excited to welcome the sunrise!

Later in the morning he'll sing more slowly, without those high screeches. We might also see robins hopping along on the lawn, cocking their heads first this way, then that, looking for a juicy earthworm for breakfast.

FACT: Robins are usually the first birds to sing in the morning.

NORTHERN CARDINAL

Cheer cheer cheer cheer

Cheer . . . Hear that soft whistle from high in the tree? Just one note. Quietly, a cardinal awakens.

In that single whistle is cardinal magic. The one *cheer* note we heard was actually two. The cardinal sings first through his right voice box and then shifts to his left voice box for the lower part. He's singing along with himself!

Now he sings the full song: *cheer cheer cheer cheer.* He repeats that same song over and over, but eventually he will offer you another of the dozen or so songs he knows. Maybe it will be more complex, sounding something like *weeet weeet weeet birdie birdie birdie.*

She sings, too! The female has learned the same songs as her mate. She often sings from her nest.

Seven states claim these gorgeous "redbirds," as they're often called, as their official state bird: Illinois, Indiana, Kentucky, North Carolina, Ohio, Virginia, and West Virginia.

FACT: The cardinal is named after the bright-red clothing of Roman Catholic cardinals.

TUFTED TITMOUSE

Peter-peter-peter

It's hard to leave a singing cardinal, but there's a new bird up ahead, out toward the edge of the park. Hear him there? *Peter-peter-peter*. There it is again, each song the same short, two-syllable *peter* phrase repeated two or three times. He has three or four different songs like that.

Now listen. Can you hear another titmouse or two in the distance? Yes, we can hear three of them now, all choosing to answer each other with the same *peter-peter-peter* song. Ornithologists who study birdsong call that *matched countersinging*. The males learn their songs from one another, so all of them sing the local dialect. This particular song occurs in this neighborhood, but just a few miles away, the songs will be slightly different.

Watch him singing up there, a gray crest on his head, black forehead and rusty sides, belting the songs out one after the other. His large dark eyes are watching you!

FACT: Titmice have great memories. They take sunflower seeds from our bird feeders and hide them to eat later.

BLUE JAY

JAAY JAAY JAAY

The Blue Jay seems really upset at something. Maybe we're too close to the nest. A second jay joins in, scolding, *JAAY JAAY*. The jays are the alarm system for all birds in the neighborhood.

Check them out with the binoculars. Start at the very top, with the blue crest on the head, then a neat dark collar. White in front and dark blue down the back, with patches of shiny blue on the wings. Beautiful!

These jays have an immense vocabulary. They can change the quality of their *JAAY* calls in so many ways, as if to express their feelings of protest, anger, or defiance. They make other sounds, like bells, whistles, or even a squeaky gate. Mysteriously, they mimic hawks, fooling even the best birdwatchers. And often, if you listen to other jays chiming in, they seem to be agreeing on what should be said.

FACT: Blue Jays sometimes go "anting." A jay may settle on an anthill, letting ants crawl all through its feathers, or hold an ant its bill and wipe itself with it.

We leave the park lawns now and head toward the forest. But first we'll pass through an abandoned orchard, with vines and bushes tangled along a fence. It's what we call *edge habitat*. Many birds make their homes here—not in the forest, not in the field, but in between.

EASTERN BLUEBIRD

Ayo ala lee . . . Alee lalo lay

Perched in an old apple tree is an Eastern Bluebird. Look at his beautiful feathers—it's said that he "carries the blue of the heavens on his back." He flutters to the ground, grabs an insect, and flies back to his perch. And then, he sings!

It's a soft warble, rich and mellow, about a second long. Notice the rhythm and pattern. Then listen carefully to the next song . . . it's a little different. Third verse? Same as the first. The fourth? Same as the second! He alternates, singing two different songs one after the other.

When the bluebird isn't singing, you might hear its simple call note: a sweet *tur-a-lee*.

FACT: Bluebirds sing with their beaks mostly closed, not wide open like most songbirds.

EASTERN TOWHEE

Drink-your-teeeeeeee!

Drink-your-teeeeeeee! . . . Somewhere in the tangled, brushy fencerow sings an Eastern Towhee. The towhee is a handsome bird the size of a big sparrow. He has several different songs, but they all sound like a version of *drink your tea* with a series of *tee* notes on the end—some are more like a stuttered *drink-your-te-te-te-te-tea*!

Look there! He's popped up from behind the fence and perches on a post. See the black hood, the bright orange streaks on his plump sides, and his bright-red eyes.

Like most songbirds, he sings with more energy at dawn. He'll switch between two or three different songs, as if eager to tell all that he knows. Mixed in among the songs is his common call note, sounding like *tow-hee*.

FACT: Towhees scratch vigorously with two feet on the ground for food, sounding like a large, scary animal in dry leaf litter.

CAROLINA WREN

TEA-KETTLE, TEA-KETTLE, TEA-KETTLE

Hidden in the tangled vines, a Carolina Wren sings. He's loud! It's as if he pumps himself up with air until he's close to bursting, and only then does the song explode from his beak.

He sings a single phrase, repeated several times. It sounds like he's chanting *tea-kettle, tea-kettle, tea-kettle*. Other variations on the song might sound like *pretty bird, pretty bird, pretty bird* or *tweedle, tweedle, tweedle*. A female listening closely might hear thirty or forty different versions of her mate's song. Wrens often learn songs from their neighbors and choose to sing matching songs to one another.

While the male does most of the singing, listen for the female, too. She sometimes responds to him with a harsh chatter.

These wrens don't migrate. In December or January, you might hear the male singing, and perhaps the female chattering back. It's a cheerful song to hear, especially in the depths of winter.

FACT: These wrens build their nests in the strangest places, such as old flowerpots, mailboxes, discarded boots, a coat pocket—you never know where!

The forest beckons: big, beautiful oaks, maples, and hickory trees. Our path will take us through the woods and across a stream, then past a pond, and through more edge habitat before returning to the park where we began.

RED-EYED VIREO

Vireo . . . virea . . . voria . . . vireo

High in the treetops sings the Red-eyed Vireo.

Just a couple of whistled notes make up each brief song, and then he pauses for a moment, as if planning the next song. It almost sounds like he's talking rather than singing, asking very brief questions and giving brief answers.

Here's a listening game—the "vireo challenge." Pick out an especially distinctive song and then count the number of other songs he sings before you hear it again. You'll most likely count to about fifteen or twenty before the vireo repeats himself. Your count tells you roughly how many different songs the vireo knows.

If you try this listening game on the different Red-eyed Vireos you encounter, you won't hear the same recognizable songs. Each vireo has his own set of songs, many of which he has *improvised*, or made up on his own.

FACT: One persistent vireo sang 22,197 songs in a single day!

WOOD THRUSH

Bup bup eee-o-lay o-leeeeeeeee

Up ahead on the trail, hidden in the shadows, waits one of the most gifted singers in North America.

Hear the simple, soft *bup bup* notes that introduce each song? Next is a brilliant, flutelike *eee-o-lay*, several lovely notes flowing together. Last is a ringing trill, like *o-leeeeeeeee*, all together making up one of the most beautiful songs in the forest.

Listen closely and you'll discover that the Wood Thrush has three to five different *eee-o-lay* phrases. In the *o-leeeeeeeee*, he expertly uses his two voices to sing two different melodies at the same time.

Much of the magic lies in not knowing what the Wood Thrush will sing next. He combines his *eee-o-lay* phrases with a dozen *o-leeeeeeeee* endings. He sings song after song, each one different from the last.

FACT: The male Wood Thrush feeds the babies in the nest so the female can quickly start a second nest to raise more young.

EASTERN PHOEBE

Fee-bree . . . fee-b-be-bee

Deep in the forest, we cross a stream on an old wooden bridge. An Eastern Phoebe announces that this is home. His mate is probably hidden under the bridge, sitting on a nest built on the bridge supports.

What do you hear? Two different songs, both simple. One is *fee-bree,* with a clear *fee* that rises and then falls, then *bree* as a lower, raspy note. He's saying his name!

The other song begins with the same *fee* but ends with a higher, stuttered series of notes, something like *fee-b-be-bee.* How many *fee-bree* songs will the phoebe offer before doing a single *fee-b-be-bee*? Just one, as in excited dawn singing? Or three or four, when more relaxed? The count tells us his mood.

The Eastern Phoebe is a kind of bird called a *flycatcher.* These birds quickly flutter from a perch to catch an insect in midair. Then they zip back to their perch, waiting to grab the next tasty bug.

FACT: The phoebe's song is not learned but innate, and all Eastern Phoebes everywhere have the same two songs.

BARRED OWL

Who cooks for you? Who cooks for you-alllll?

Beyond the bridge, our path turns to follow the meandering stream. Here in the deep forest is the home of a pair of Barred Owls.

These night-calling owls are silent now. But if we had been here in the middle of the night, we would have heard them ask the question *Who cooks for you? Who cooks for you-alllll?* It's eight hoots in all. The final note ends with a *vibrato,* a shaky, quavering sound. The female's voice is higher pitched and has a longer vibrato note.

Sometimes the owls will give a long *whooooooo-allllllllll,* or a series of *who* notes followed by the familiar *allll*: *who who who who who who-alllll.*

And sometimes the owls just seem to go crazy! They bark and cackle and gurgle and shriek and whoop and hoot and caw, with just enough *cook* and *who-all* notes thrown in to give them away. Even if you are prepared for it, your hair will stand on end.

FACT: Unlike most bird species, the females are larger than the male. On a seesaw (or teeter-totter), three females on one end would balance four males on the other.

We leave the forest behind and stop at the pond, with dense tangles of cattails along the shoreline. Dead trees ring the pond, as if they have been drowned by high water. And here are some benches, where we can sit, watch, and listen.

RED-WINGED BLACKBIRD

Konk-la-reeeeee

A Red-winged Blackbird sounds upset that we're here, calling loudly with a piercing *tee-err*. Eventually he accepts our presence and settles down, and he sings: *konk-la-reeeeee*, beginning with several low gurgling notes followed by a higher buzzy trill.

Like the cardinal, titmouse, towhee, and Carolina Wren, he repeats one of his songs many times before revealing another of the half dozen that he knows. As he sings, he spreads his tail and wings, almost falling forward off his perch, showing off brilliant red wing patches against his jet-black *plumage*, or feathers. He's not showing off for us, but for a female somewhere in the tangled brush below him.

There she is! Flying out of a cattail clump, calling sharply in flight, *ch-ch-ch-ch-ch-chit-chit*.

After a few minutes, she returns, calling softly. She works her way back to her nest deep in the cattails' shelter.

FACT: During the winter, blackbirds roost together in marshes at night, sometimes with more than a million birds.

COMMON YELLOWTHROAT

Wich-i-ty wich-i-ty wich-i-ty

Now another voice sings from the cattail tangles. It's the yellowthroat, warbling a gentle *wich-i-ty wich-i-ty wich-i-ty*, a three-syllable phrase repeated several times. This is the only melody he knows.

Cup your hands to your ears and listen for other yellowthroats. Several of them hold territories in the pond habitat, and when they sing, we can hear how songs vary from bird to bird. Some might sing a two-syllable *witch-y*, or a four-syllable *wich-a-we-o*. Their songs duel with each other in the spring sunrise.

Quick! There he is, top of the cattail, but not for long. With that black mask, he looks like a bandit. See the bright-yellow throat? You can see how this bird got its name.

FACT: The yellowthroat is a warbler, and warblers are such pretty birds that a flock of them is sometimes called a "bouquet."

NORTHERN FLICKER

Wik-wik-wik-wik-wik-wik . . .

From out beyond the edge of the pond, among tall dead trees, comes a drumbeat of rapid-fire sounds. It's a woodpecker, banging his beak against the tree at about twenty-five blows per second. He's drumming, announcing this is his territory.

Let's listen for clues to figure out which woodpecker it is. . . . There it is: a Northern Flicker, with a loud, ringing song, *wik-wik-wik-wik-wik-wik-wik*, with seven or so *wik* notes each second.

Now he flies, showing bright glints of yellow in his wings. He flies in typical woodpecker roller-coaster flight, alternating wing flaps with a torpedolike glide, when he folds his wings against his body. Then he lands on the side of a tall tree, propping himself against the trunk with stiff tail feathers.

And why the name "flicker"? Early in the spring, during courtship, three or four birds may gather on a tree trunk. They bob and dance, excitedly calling *FLICK-a FLICK-a FLICK-a*.

FACT: The flicker's tongue is long, extending far beyond the beak to collect ants. When not in use, the tongue is stored in a long tube that wraps around the skull.

It's wonderful sitting here on the bench, but we should be moving along. A few more birds await us on the way back to the park. First, we cross a brushy field.

INDIGO BUNTING

Fire fire where where heeerre my my run run faster faster safe safe pheeewww

From the top of a tree up ahead sings an Indigo Bunting. He's a dazzling bright blue, and in just the right light you might see that his head is a little purplish.

Feel the rhythm—that's the key to remembering his song. He almost always sings in twos: two of this, then two of that, giving equal time to each pair of sounds. Over a few seconds, the song gets lower and quieter. Song after song, always the same. The Indigo Bunting is another songbird in which each male has only one song.

Off to the right sings another Indigo Bunting. As they sing back and forth, compare their songs. It's like one is an echo of the other! These two Indigo Buntings live in a small community where they have learned their songs from each other. Not far away, even in the next field over, the buntings' songs could be all different.

FACT: A cardinal is red because it has red pigments in its feathers, but birds like the Indigo Bunting that are blue do not have blue pigments. Instead, when light enters the feathers, because of the structure of the feathers, only blue wavelengths escape to our eyes.

MOURNING DOVE

Coowah cooo coo coo

A Mourning Dove flutters from the path ahead. As his wings cut the air, they make a whistling sound.

A short distance away he lands and sings. Listen—he's telling us how he got his name. It's a mournful song, low and slow: *coowah cooo coo coo*. It sounds a lot like an owl. The first phrase is two syllables, slurred upward, the *wah* stressed; the following *coo* notes are shorter and slurred slightly down. The song is innate, so Mourning Doves everywhere have the same song.

Just a few songs, and he's quiet again. He must already have a mate. If not, he would be singing all morning long in his attempt to attract a partner.

You can listen for their whistling wings all winter, as Mourning Doves often come to birdfeeders. Not until spring approaches, however, might you hear the nonstop song of a male advertising for a mate: *coowah cooo coo coo.*

FACT: Mourning Dove parents regurgitate (spit up!) a white goo, called "pigeon milk," for their tiniest babies.

NORTHERN MOCKINGBIRD

Pete-pete-pete-pete-pete-repeat!

Just beyond the Mourning Dove, in the shady woods, we can hear the ultimate songbird: the Northern Mockingbird! His scientific name, *Mimus polyglottos*, translates to "many-tongued mimic." He has an amazing ability to copy the songs of other birds. He starts off with the phoebe's stutter song . . . then sings the songs of the Carolina Wren. He copies the lovely melody of the Wood Thrush, the whistle of the cardinal, and the harsh calls of the Blue Jay. He's a feathered choir all by himself. He loves the sounds of car alarms and cell phone ringtones, too!

And if the singer is a bachelor, without a mate? He will sing not only all day, but also through much of the night.

Try the "vireo challenge" with a mockingbird, counting from one example of a distinctive song to the next, and you'll likely count to one hundred or more songs over several minutes.

FACT: The female sings, too, especially when she establishes her own territory for the winter.

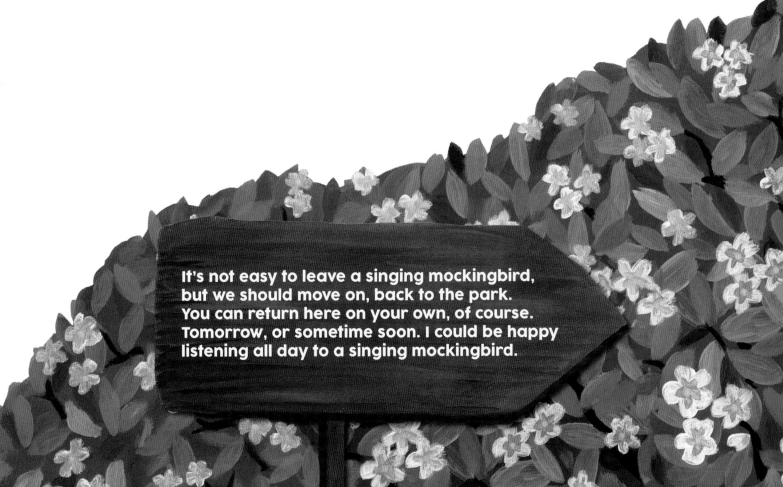

It's not easy to leave a singing mockingbird, but we should move on, back to the park. You can return here on your own, of course. Tomorrow, or sometime soon. I could be happy listening all day to a singing mockingbird.

CHIPPING SPARROW

Chip-chip-chip-chip-chip-chip-chip-chip

We're almost back to where we started, but there are still a few more singers to hear. There's an interesting, rattling song in the tree overhead. It's a Chipping Sparrow, whose song consists of a simple *chip* note, repeated for a few seconds. That's it! That's the one song he knows.

But the next Chipping Sparrow might have a different song. It will also consist of a single sound repeated many times, but that sound could be longer and sweeter. Occasionally, you'll hear two neighboring males with the same songs. That's because one bird learned the song of his neighbor, just as Indigo Buntings do.

At dawn, three or four males often gather on the ground, where they spit ultra-brief songs, up to sixty each minute, and race about, challenging each other. When the dawn skirmishes are over, each bird returns to his own territory, where he sings high in the trees.

FACT: Like many small songbirds, this sparrow weighs far less than a fun-size candy bar—about the weight of four pennies.

EUROPEAN STARLING

Pops, clicks, rattles, squeaks, chirps, twitters, warbles, screams, gurgles!

A starling hops around in the grass on the edge of the parking lot. He's *foraging*, looking for insects and other invertebrates by probing into the ground with his long yellow beak.

Another starling sings overhead, from a maple tree. What an amazing sequence of odd sounds! For most of a minute he carries on, becoming more excited, throwing his whole body into the performance. He quivers and sways, singing his heart out until the frantic wing-waving finale.

Here's the next song. What did you hear? There's the *wik-wik* song of the flicker . . . and the *fee-bree* of the phoebe. Like their relatives the mockingbirds, starlings are good at mimicking the songs of other birds.

Here's the amazing part: the starling mimicked the flicker and phoebe simultaneously, using his left voice to mimic one sound, and the right to mimic the other. Only starlings are known to juggle two mimicked sounds at once like this!

FACT: Starlings came from Europe, introduced to North America in the late 1800s. Now they're everywhere!

HOUSE FINCH

A rollicking, cheerful warbling . . . Veeeer

That first robin we heard seems so long ago, and now it's almost time for lunch. Let's go sit on the porch at the visitor center.

Do you see what's happening at that hanging flowerpot at the other end of the porch? A sparrow-sized bird disappears into the flowers . . . and then reappears and flies away. All brownish with heavy streaks on the breast. It's the female House Finch, who has hidden her nest among the flowers.

Her mate sings nearby. It's a friendly, cheery song, starting high and gently descending over two to three seconds. The lively notes are interrupted with a husky, down-slurred *veeeer*, usually at the end of the song.

Those last bright and friendly chirps from the House Finch are a nice way to end our listening adventure!

FACT: All eastern House Finches, now found from the Atlantic to the Great Plains, are descended from a few California birds released in New York City in 1939.

WESTERN NORTH AMERICA

ANOTHER DAWN WALK

It's time for another early morning walk. We'll follow a similar trail, from a park on the edge of town to the woods and back again. We'll recognize a few of the songs we hear: these belong to birds that live in both eastern and western North America. But we're going to meet many new birds and hear many new songs along our way.

GREAT HORNED OWL

Who who-ooo whooo whoo

Listen! The hoot owls are still awake. They've been up all night, catching mice in the dark to feed their babies in the nest. Well, mostly mice. Sometimes it's something bigger, like a rabbit.

There! *Who who-ooo whooo whoo.* Like a foghorn in the distance. All the notes are on the same pitch, and always in the same rhythm.

Listen again. Do you hear a second owl, like an echo, answering the first? This is special. The female is nearby and calls first with the higher-pitched hoots; he then answers with hoots that are even lower.

With that hooked beak and strong talons, this owl is a fearsome predator. The "horns" are only tufts of feathers, but they give a fierce look. The owl can turn its head to look behind itself, and those enormous yellow eyes have excellent night vision and allow the owl to see everything.

FACT: The disc of feathers on the owl's face helps funnel sound to its sharp ears.

WESTERN WOOD-PEWEE

Bzeeyeer, tswee-tee-teet

The first singing bird begins in the treetop overhead: an occasional *bzeeyeer*—short, simple, the first half buzzy, the last half dropping in pitch. *Bzeeyeer . . . bzeeyeer . . .* He almost sounds sad, or worried, but that's only how we hear the song, of course, not how he feels.

Hear his other song? He stutters a rising *tswee-tee-teet.* Now he's alternating two songs, *bzeeyeer, tswee-tee-teet, bzeeyeer, tswee-teeteet,* singing thirty to forty songs each minute. It's as if he asks a question on the rising *tswee-tee-teet* and then quickly answers with *bzeeyeer,* but he's never satisfied with his answer. Eventually, maybe fifteen minutes before sunrise, he'll stop this dawn singing. Then you'll hear only his *bzeeyeer* throughout the day. His songs are innate, not learned from other birds, so they are the same everywhere.

He's a "sit-and-wait" predator, a flycatcher like the Eastern Phoebe, perching until an insect flies by, then sallying out to catch it before returning to the perch.

FACT: The pewee's name comes from the song of its eastern cousin, the Eastern Wood-Pewee: *pee-wee.*

AMERICAN ROBIN

Cheerily, cheer-up, cheerio, cheerily eek

Two to three hours ago, the first robins began singing beside the Atlantic Ocean. Since then, their songs have swept across the continent until this minute, when the dawn wave of their songs has reached us.

Hear him move quickly among those strong, low notes: *cheerily, cheer-up, cheerio, cheerily*. We often say a robin "carols," which means "sings happily." After several of those low carols, listen for a high screech, like an *eek*. Later in the day, when he's less excited, he'll sing just the low carols.

Listen carefully to each carol. At first, no two may sound alike, but eventually you may hear a carol that is especially different from the others. How soon do you hear it again? If you had the ears of a robin, you'd be able to identify a dozen or more different carols that each robin offers.

When the sun rises, we'll see our robins running along the ground, cocking their heads, searching for earthworms.

FACT: During winter, especially if the ground is frozen, robins eat mostly fruit instead of earthworms.

YELLOW WARBLER

Sweet sweet sweet I'm so sweet

There's another excited dawn singer, over in the willows beside the stream. He calls frantically, *chip chip chip-chip*, then delivers a bright, emphatic song, about a second long. The clear, whistled notes rise and fall rapidly, *sweet sweet sweet I'm so sweet*. Then it's more calling, so much calling it seems that he sometimes forgets to sing.

If you had the ear of a Yellow Warbler, you'd hear that he sings about a dozen different songs at dawn. Give it a try! Concentrate on the pattern and rhythm of one song and compare it to the next, and that one to the next, and so on.

It's still too dark to see well, but imagine him sitting there. He's a bright splash of yellow, with rusty streaks on his bright-yellow breast. His beady black eye probably sees us. He throws his head back, working his throat and bill as he offers his song to the world.

FACT: Sometimes a cowbird lays an egg in a Yellow Warbler nest. The warblers don't eject the egg but instead start another nest on top of the cowbird egg.

Beyond the park, we'll find more birds up ahead in the low, scrubby transition between open parkland and the forest. It's what we call *edge habitat*. Edges like this are often rich in birdlife.

HOUSE WREN

A stuttering and bubbling and gurgling gush of energy

On the edge of the park, someone has nailed a bird house to a tree. Just above it, a House Wren sings. Just listen to him gurgle and bubble. He begins with a few low, stuttered chatters, then suddenly explodes into higher notes before falling back down the scale. He hardly has time to take a breath before he sings again, and again.

And should a female show some interest in him? He goes into hyperdrive, singing nonstop near her, his entire body shaking and fluffing with the performance. Once she's laid her eggs in his nest box, he'll likely find another nest box and try to attract another female there.

Watch him sing. See the tail cocked over his back. The bill opens and closes rapidly as he delivers the song, the entire body seeming to shake violently with all his effort.

FACT: The Chippewa people call the House Wren *O-du-na'-mis-sug-ud-da-we'-shi*, which translates to "big noise for its size."

MOURNING DOVE

Coowah cooo coo coo

See up ahead beside the path, the bird perched in the dead branches of the small tree? Its head is small, its tail long and pointed. He sings, *coowah cooo coo coo*, low and slow, sounding even sadder than the pewee we heard earlier. Feel the rhythm, the long note that rises, then three notes that fall slightly. All Mourning Doves sound like this, because their song is innate. The dove is named for how we hear it: the "mourning" dove.

Off he flies. Do you hear the whistling in the wings? It's not a merry song, but it's a pleasant sound that the wing feathers make as they whisk the bird away from us.

Mourning Doves are everywhere, from the Atlantic to the Pacific, and from Canada down into Mexico. Just like people! In fact, there are about as many Mourning Doves as there are people in Canada and the United States.

FACT: "Two turtle-doves" in the song "The Twelve Days of Christmas" is just right, because a male and female dove typically mate for life.

NORTHERN FLICKER

FLICK-a FLICK-a FLICK-a

We walk on, and up from the path flies a Northern Flicker. See the big white spot on its back just above the tail? See how the wings flash red with each wing beat? The reddish color is fascinating. The eastern form of the Northern Flicker has yellow in the wings, the western form, red. In the Great Plains, such as Nebraska, the feather colors change. Some birds there have orange feathers—they are *hybrids*.

See it perched there on the dead tree? The red moustache on its face tells us it's a male. He sings, *wik-wik-wik-wik-wik-wik-wik*. And drums, slamming his beak into the tree about twenty-five times each second. A loud call, *klee-yer*, often tells that flickers are near. The flicker is named for its courtship calls, which sound like *FLICK-a FLICK-a FLICK-a*.

Here's a good word: *zygodactyl*. It means "two toes in front and two behind." This arrangement lets woodpeckers climb trees better than the more usual three in front, one behind arrangement (which is *anisodactyl*— ornithologists love big words!).

FACT: If the flicker's head were as big as ours, it could stick its long tongue out about a foot. Imagine that!

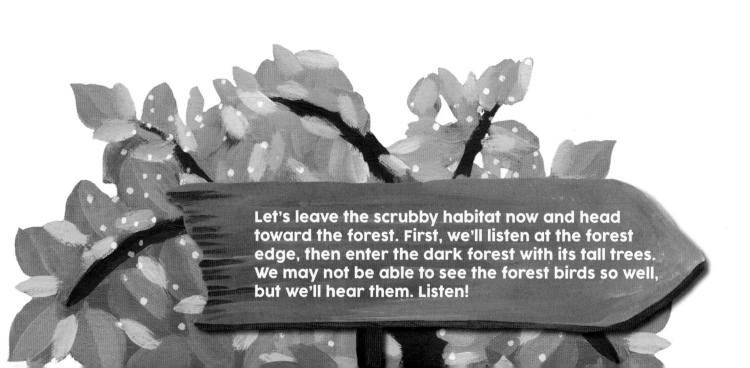

Let's leave the scrubby habitat now and head toward the forest. First, we'll listen at the forest edge, then enter the dark forest with its tall trees. We may not be able to see the forest birds so well, but we'll hear them. Listen!

BLACK-HEADED GROSBEAK

A robin who has had voice lessons!

There! A gloriously beautiful robin-like song! The robin leaves a slight pause between the separate notes of his song: *cheerily, cheer-up, cheerio, cheerily*. Not so the grosbeak. He glides expertly from one note to the next, with no small pauses.

The entire song is a masterpiece, a rich melody of whistles that slur high and low. After several seconds he does pause, as if taking some time to admire his genius. And then he's at it again . . . and again.

In the spring, he sings all day until he attracts a mate. Once his mate has laid her eggs, he takes his turn incubating them, and he sings from the nest, too. He can't stop.

Sometimes the only clue that a grosbeak is near is their sharp *chink* call, sounding like the squeak of a rubber shoe on a gym floor.

FACT: As their name suggests, grosbeaks have large beaks. All the better to crack the large, hard seeds they eat.

WESTERN TANAGER

A robin with a sore throat!

Near the grosbeak, there's another confusing robin-like song, from the Western Tanager. Hear him up there, sounding a bit like a robin, a bit like a grosbeak? There's a hoarse quality to the songs, though, as if a robin has a sore throat. And that's how we recognize the tanager.

He's a dashing red and black and yellow, with a touch of white in the wing. The female is here somewhere, too, but dressed more in camouflaged yellowish green, like sunlight shining on green leaves.

During the day his songs are about two seconds long, consisting of five to seven burry notes, and then he pauses for maybe five seconds. At dawn, he sings continuously, but at half speed, and every few seconds he interjects his *pit-er-ick* call, a split-second dry, rising rattle. The *pit-er-ick* call is also used later in the day, when the tanager seems disturbed at something.

FACT: The red in the male's feathers comes from red pigments in certain insects that he eats.

BROWN-HEADED COWBIRD

Bublowcomseeee or *Bub-ko-lum-tseeee*
or *Glug glug glee*

See the three birds at the top of that dead tree? They take turns singing. The singer fluffs his feathers, spreads his wings, and nearly falls forward off his perch as he sings. They're a glossy black with brown heads.

They are Brown-headed Cowbirds. It's a bird many people love to hate: they are *brood parasites*, which means that the females lay their eggs in the nests of other species.

How do you hear them? *Bublowcomseeee*? *Glug glug glee*? The mnemonics aren't very flattering, but that's because our ears can't hear the song's special effects. Listen carefully and you'll first hear a few really low gurgling notes. Those are from his left voice box. Then, in a split second, he switches to his right voice box and leaps to sounds so high we strain to hear them.

Away they go! Hear that hissy whistle as they fly? It's their "flight whistle," maybe sounding something like *whsssss-pseeee*.

FACT: These birds are called "cowbirds" because they are often found searching on the ground for insects stirred up by cattle.

HERMIT THRUSH

Ooooooooooooh, holy holy, ah, purity purity, eeh, sweetly sweetly

We step into the dark forest now. . . .

A Hermit Thrush sings, some of nature's best music. Hear how he begins his songs with a pure tone just a half-second long? Then, using his two voice boxes, he whirls and twirls through his fluty ending. It's like he sings on a trampoline, one song high, then one low, then one in between. He leaps about the musical scale, always with the next song different from the one he just sang.

He has about ten different songs, and he usually sings them all in a row before starting over again. When you hear his highest song, listen for him to sing it again. You'll hear it about every ten songs.

Birds in the thrush family are some of our favorite singers. In the East, Wood Thrushes and Eastern Bluebirds are special, and the American Robin can be enjoyed across the entire continent.

FACT: The Hermit Thrush is often the last bird to sing before nightfall. Listen for him on a quiet summer evening between sunset and dark.

With the thrush's lovely song still in our ears, we leave the forest now and walk beside a stream bordered with willow thickets.

SPOTTED TOWHEE

Your-teeeeeeeeeeeee! or Chweeeeeeee

A male Spotted Towhee perches in the bush by the stream, looking us over with his red eyes. Except for all the white spots on his black wing, he looks like his close relative the Eastern Towhee—both are black with reddish (or *rufous*) sides and a white belly.

Zhreeee. He calls, a simple rising growl. Not yet singing, but let's wait. . . . *Chweeeeeeee.* There's his song, a buzzy trill, about a second long. He continues singing, the same *chweeeeeeee* about every ten seconds. We count them, five, ten, twelve! Then, an entirely different song, like *Your tetetetetetete.* If we're quick, we can count the number of *te* notes. He knows about half a dozen different songs. During the day, he sings lazily with what we call *eventual variety*—meaning he sings one song several times before switching to another. But during the dawn hour, he switches excitedly between different songs one after the other. We call this *immediate variety.*

FACT: The two towhees are so similar that expert ornithologists have often wondered if they should be called one species, the Rufous-sided Towhee, or two, the Spotted Towhee and Eastern Towhee.

WHITE-CROWNED SPARROW

Seeeeeeee sitli-sitli te-te-te-te-te-zrrrrr

There's a fine song, coming from the other side of the willow. A White-crowned Sparrow. He begins with a raspy whistle, *seeeeeeee*, followed by two slower notes, *sitli-sitli*, then a rapid trill, *te-te-te-te-te*, and he punctuates his song with a down-slurred *zrrrrr*.

That's his song, the only one he knows. Listen to him repeat it. Then listen up ahead on the path. Do you hear another bird with the same song? Yes, all the White-crowned Sparrows here will sing in the same dialect.

But travel some distance and you'll hear a different dialect. In the mountains, White-crowned Sparrows in different meadows have different dialects. In the chaparral along the Pacific Ocean, you can walk from one dialect to the next. In some places, you can even stand on the boundary between two dialects: to your left you hear one dialect, to your right, another.

FACT: A young White-crowned Sparrow learns his song in the dialect where he settles to raise his family.

RED-WINGED BLACKBIRD

Konk-la-reeeeee

See the bird perching on the fence post in front of us, all black with a red patch on his wing? A male Red-winged Blackbird.

The female is completely different—she's a reddish brown with dark streaks on her breast. And a one-year-old male can look a lot like her, or be all black with only a little red.

Each older male holds a territory here and sings *konk-la-reeeeee*. He also seems to call constantly with a variety of similar notes, like *check, chuck, chink, chunk, chick*, sometimes an ear-shattering *tee-err*. She doesn't sing but calls as she goes about her nesting business. Her *ch-ch-ch-ch-ch-chit-chit* call answers the singing male who owns the territory where she nests.

It's a complex society. Several females might nest in the territory of each male. The father of a mother's babies might be the territory owner—or a male from a neighboring territory. And the male who owns the territory? He has some babies with females on his territory and some babies with females on neighboring territories. Ornithologists call such a mating system *polygynandrous*.

FACT: When the male sings, he often shows off his red "epaulets" by spreading his wings, almost falling forward off the perch as he does so.

BARN SWALLOW

Musical twittering with dry, creaking rattles

We come to a bridge over the stream. Swarming all about are Barn Swallows. Under the bridge we can see their mud nests on the supports. There's a bird down by the stream collecting mud for its nest. Others fly in and out, delivering food to their babies.

One male perches in the bushes off to the side of the commotion. What fun listening to his jumbled, bubbling thrill of a song. It's a superspeed roller coaster of notes that run high and low. And then there's a most peculiar sound, a dry, creaking rattle. It almost sounds like he's laughing, but really fast.

And off he flies, calling *vit . . . vit-vit* on the wing. Do you see how his tail is forked, with the outer tail feathers much longer than the inner ones?

FACT: The Barn Swallow once nested mostly in caves, but they have now almost entirely adopted human-made structures for their nesting—including, of course, barns.

The stream leads us back toward the park. But first we'll pass through a meadow, where we'll find—and hear—birds that prefer open spaces.

RED-TAILED HAWK

Kee-eeee-arrr

Listen! It sounds like a scream, coming from somewhere up high. There it is, a Red-tailed Hawk, wings stretched out, soaring high over the field. The color of the tail feathers tell you how this hawk got its name.

Again it calls, *kee-eeee-arrr.* About two to three seconds, a bit hoarse and shrill, slurred down. Doesn't it sound fierce and powerful? Maybe you've heard this sound before—in the movies! The Red-tailed Hawk itself is almost never in the movies, but its *kee-eeee-arrr* is. Because it feels powerful and hair-raising, the red-tail's *kee-eeee-arrr* is sometimes used as the sound effect for big, powerful eagles.

Watch for these hawks perched in trees along the road. They sit and wait patiently, watching alertly for a mouse down below. Wait long enough and you may see the hawk fly down to the ground to grab its meal.

FACT: Red-tailed Hawk parents take turns incubating their eggs, for about a month. Small songbirds incubate their eggs for only about ten days.

WESTERN MEADOWLARK

Short, rich whistles ending in a rush

There's the song of a Western Meadowlark. See him far up ahead, sitting on the fence post?

He begins with short, rich whistles, pronounced with great care, low and slow enough that our ears can savor them. He then hurries into a fast, bubbling jumble of notes to end his song.

Hear how he repeats the same song over and over? Do you hear other meadowlarks singing in the distance? Yes, they're all talking to each other. Now our meadowlark changes his song. He's another bird who sings with eventual variety, and he knows about half a dozen different songs.

As we walk slowly toward him, he calls, *vicicicicicicic*, sounding mildly alarmed, and flies off into the distance.

How did this bird get its name? It lives in open fields, or meadows. And although it belongs to the blackbird family, including the Red-winged Blackbird and Brown-headed Cowbird, its songs are so beautiful that they remind some people of one of the most special European songbirds, the skylark.

FACT: Six states claim the Western Meadowlark as their state bird: Kansas, Montana, Nebraska, North Dakota, Oregon, and Wyoming.

COMMON RAVEN

Deep *Croak* or hoarse *Rrronk*

Rrronk! In the distance, there's a raven flying toward us, a big all-black bird, about the size of a Red-tailed Hawk. *Rrronk.* The raven is the biggest of the five thousand different songbirds in the world. And probably the smartest, too. *Rrronk.* The raven is full of superlatives.

The raven lands on a utility pole up ahead. Perhaps it is just curious about us. Ravens have also learned that humans can mean food, so it could be looking for a meal.

He's changed his tune to a quiet, two-syllable *ka-ronk.* And he seems to be talking to himself, muttering soft raven-speak between *ka-ronk*s.

A second raven calls from the distance: *croak.* Our raven responds with its own deep *croak.* That's typical raven talk. Listen carefully and you might hear a pair of ravens calling to each other in the same voice. They often match each other like songbirds do with their songs.

FACT: Sometimes ravens do somersaults in the air, or even fly upside-down. Sometimes they slide down snowbanks on their backs. As if just for fun!

Now we're leaving the wild, open meadow behind and returning to the tended space of the town park. We'll find one or two more birds here to listen to, before our morning walk is over.

HOUSE FINCH

A rollicking, cheerful warbling... Veeeer

It's hard to think unhappy thoughts when the House Finches are singing. And sing they do, as several pairs are nesting in the small junipers here beside the parking lot.

It's a lively song, bouncing high and low, often including a harsh, down-slurred *veeeer* note, sometimes in the middle of the song, sometimes at the end.

How excited the male becomes when courting a female. He stands tall and faces her, singing continuously with high squeaky notes added to his songs.

See the reddish color in the male's feathers on his head and breast? He's red like that because he eats certain plant foods containing red pigments called *carotenoids*. Some males are more yellow than red because they eat foods with different pigments.

Once, House Finches nested mainly in the hot deserts of the Southwest. Now they're everywhere, from the Atlantic to the Pacific. The millions of eastern finches are all descended from a few birds released in New York City in 1939.

FACT: With the male's reddish feathers, the House Finch was given the scientific name *Haemorhous mexicanus*, from the Greek word *haemo*, which means "blood," and because it was first described in Mexico.

ANNA'S HUMMINGBIRD

*Bzzbzzbzz bzzbzzbzz bzzbzzbzz chur-ZWEE
dzi!dzi!*

There's an Anna's Hummingbird, a little winged jewel.
Just look at him eyeing us from his perch atop that
bush. The feathers on his head and neck are magically
iridescent, flashing a bright rosy color when the sun
shines on him just right. Then he turns away, and his
head can appear yellow or even black.

And how he sings, a scratchy sputtering so high and
fast that our ears can't appreciate it. A series of triple
buzzes, *bzzbzzbzz*, some dainty notes in the middle of the
song, *chur-ZWEE*, ending with a couple of harsh notes
again, *dzi!dzi!* A young male learns his song from adult
singers, in the local dialect.

Up he flies, maybe thirty yards. Then he dives almost
straight down, as fast as sixty miles per hour, before he
suddenly pulls up with a buzz and a squeak.

FACT: The whirr you can hear when a hummingbird is
near is the sound of its wings beating the air about fifty
times each second.

BIRDSONG GLOSSARY

brood parasites: Birds (or other animals), such as the Brown-headed Cowbird, that rely on other species to raise their offspring.

call: Relatively simple sounds made by female and male birds of all ages, to coordinate their lives, warn of danger, and the like.

common name: The name given to a bird species by which it is most often, or "commonly" known. It is a proper noun, and therefore usually capitalized. See also *scientific name*.

countersinging: When two singers "duel" with their songs, sometimes taking turns singing, sometimes overlapping each other.

dialect: Learned songs, sometimes calls, used by birds at a given location, differing from those sounds used by birds of the same species at some distance away.

duet: Two birds, usually a male and female, singing or calling together, sometimes in precise patterns, other times more loosely.

eventual variety: When a bird that knows several different songs offers one of his songs several times before switching to another. See also *immediate variety*.

genus: A group of closely related bird species that are similar to each other. See also *species*.

hybrid: The offspring when the mother and father are from different species or varieties of animals, as in flickers.

immediate variety: When a bird that knows several songs sings different songs one after the other. See also *eventual variety*.

innate song: A song that is not learned. Innate songs vary little from one individual of the same species to the next. Examples include the Mourning Dove, Barred Owl, Northern Flicker, Eastern Phoebe.

larynx: The voice box of a mammal, including humans, found at the top of the windpipe. See also *syrinx*.

learned song: A song that is learned from listening to the songs of other birds of the same species. Many birds, especially songbirds, have the ability to listen to a song, memorize it, and then sing it. See also *mimicry*.

matched countersinging: A form of *countersinging*, when two birds (usually males) with several songs in their repertoire choose the same learned song to sing back and forth at each other.

mimicry: The ability of some birds, such as a Northern Mockingbird, to mimic the sounds of another species.

repertoire: The variety of songs that a bird can perform. A Chipping Sparrow has just one song, but a Red-winged Blackbird may have a repertoire of half a dozen songs.

scientific name: The technical name of a bird species, used by ornithologists and other scientists. Usually consists of two words, the *genus* and *species* names, often derived from Latin or Greek.

song: A relatively loud and often complex series of "musical" notes or sounds, usually made by the male. See also *call*.

songbird: A general term for any bird that sings, but one that ornithologists use to refer to "true songbirds," which have an especially complex syrinx and a special brain for learning songs.

species: Birds of one kind, the most basic unit of classification; birds of one kind breed with each other but not with other species.

syrinx: The voice box of a bird, found at the bottom of the windpipe, where it branches to the two lungs. Consists of a voice box at the top of each branch, so that birds can sing with two voices at the same time. See also *larynx*.

vocabulary: All the sounds made by a particular bird.

VARIETY IN BIRDSONG

Some birds sound the same everywhere—for example, the Mourning Dove, Barred Owl, Northern Flicker, and Eastern Phoebe. Songs of these bird are *innate*, with the songs determined by their genes. The song genes are the same everywhere, so the songs are, too. The Eastern Phoebe always has the same two songs, *fee-bree* and *fee-b-be-bee*. That's it. Learning to recognize the songs of these species is the easiest.

Others can be difficult. These are songbirds that learn songs, just like we learn to speak. Each Chipping Sparrow has only one song, for example, but each bird can learn a different song. Their remarkable variety often stumps even the experts. You need to hear many different Chipping Sparrows before you can begin to really know them.

Song *dialects* are a challenge, too. Songs that you learn at one location might all be different from those sung by the same species at another place not all that far away. Indigo Buntings are an example.

Then there are big *repertoires*. Some singers have a large collection of different songs. Both female and male Northern Cardinals have about a dozen different songs, all of a local dialect. Carolina Wrens may sing forty different songs, Northern Mockingbirds, a hundred or more.

Still, there are rules and patterns for each species. All singers of a species have the same theme, we might say, but with variations. The Common Yellowthroat has his *wich-i-ty*, the Eastern Towhee his *drink-your-teeeeeeee*, the Red-eyed Vireo his *vireo*. Learn the general pattern, then listen to more examples. You'll be well on your way to knowing which species is which when you hear it.

BIRDSONG IS SEASONAL

Winter is very quiet—ornithologists call it the Big Silence. But when our calendar says the "first day of winter" on December 21, the days start getting longer. The birds who winter with us, like the Carolina Wren in the East, take note. They begin singing more. They know our first day of winter as their first day of spring!

And then the migrants return! That's in April in the southern part of North America, May in the North. Bird lovers head to the woods, to the swamps, everywhere to listen for them. The males arrive first and sing all day long, for a week or more. Then the females arrive and choose their mates. Nesting begins, and already it's quieter. With the nest built, eggs are laid, and babies hatch. They need a lot of food, and Mom and Dad work overtime to keep the kids healthy.

By July or August, it seems very quiet again, unless you listen closely. Then you can hear young birds, maybe just six weeks old, already practicing their songs. It's mostly the males, and they babble, just like we humans do when we're toddlers.

And then the migrants are gone. The residents, those that stay with us, don't sing much then, if at all. They use calls. Both female and male mockingbirds, for example, call harshly at dawn and dusk from their overnight roosts. We lovers of birdsong await December 21—and especially the return of singing migrants in spring.

DOES A BIRD SING BECAUSE IT'S HAPPY?

We'd like to think so, partly because we're happy to hear the song. It's often remarkably beautiful music. But there are some problems with saying a bird sings because it's happy.

The first is this: male birds sing the most when they are trying to attract a female. It's hard to suppose a male is the happiest when he's alone and desperately trying to attract a partner.

Then there's the female who, in most species, doesn't sing. If birds sing because they're happy, the females are pretty unhappy! That's no good.

And are the singers happy only during the nesting season, when they sing a lot, and unhappy the rest of the year? No, that doesn't work. We quickly realize that we can't say that "birds sing for joy."

That doesn't mean there can't be some satisfaction in a well-crafted tune or a marathon performance, or just the act of singing itself. When we humans sing, feel-good chemicals called *endorphins* are released into our brains, making us happy. Birds might experience the same kind of pleasure.

LISTENING WITH YOUR EYES

If you play a musical instrument, you are probably familiar with musical scores created for humans. We can also create musical scores for birdsong. Our eyes then become ear-openers, because we see what our ears should be hearing! We can use our eyes to train our ears.

The fancy name for a musical score for birdsong is a *spectrogram*. They're read just like human scores, from left to right, with high notes high on the score, low notes low.

Here's an example. This is a spectrogram for a Chipping Sparrow.

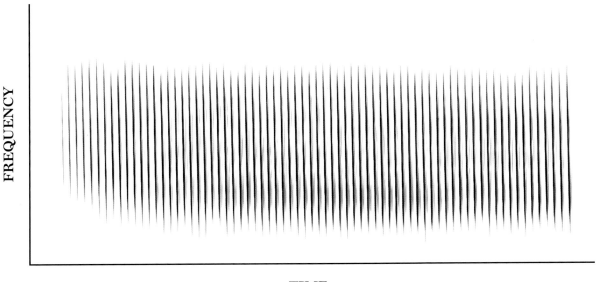

FREQUENCY

TIME

From left to right is about three seconds. Look at all those *chips*! There are about two dozen each second. And they're all the same. It's a simple song.

Up and down is *frequency*—the same as in human music. Frequency is measured in thousands of cycles per second. Middle C on a piano, for example, vibrates the air 262 times in a second, or 262 Hertz (Hz). The highest note on a piano is 4,186 Hz, the piano cord vibrating that many times each second. Many birdsongs reach up one more octave, up to 8,000 Hz, which is still well within our range of hearing. This sparrow song ranges from 4,000 to 7,000 Hz.

How about this spectrogram of a Common Yellowthroat. Do you see the repeating, three-syllable *wich-i-ty wich-i-ty wich-i-ty*? See how he adds an extra *wich* on the end?

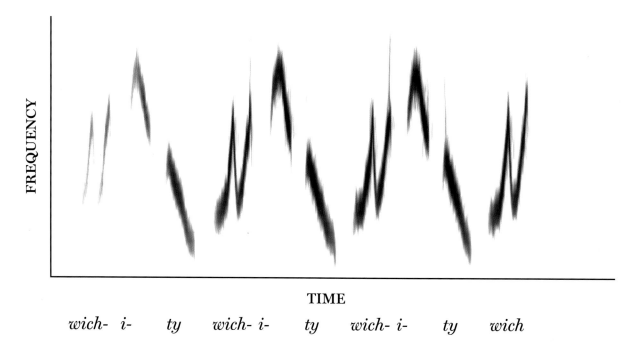

TIME

wich- i-   ty   wich- i-   ty   wich- i-   ty   wich

The spectrogram below is part of a Wood Thrush song. The first part is clear and pure, with slow whistled notes—so beautiful. Then look at the last half of the song. See that row of notes down low? Those notes are coming from the thrush's left voice box. At the same time, from the right voice box, he delivers four fast, high notes for every low note. To make the song, his brain sends messages down the nerves on each side of the neck to each side of the voice box. His breathing is precisely controlled on the left and right to produce this pattern.

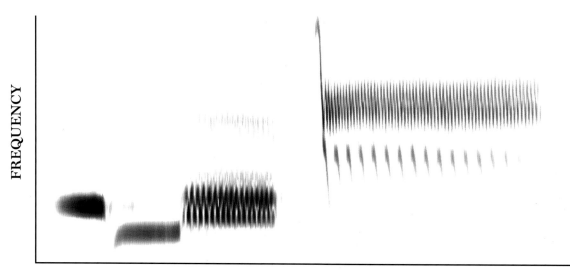

TIME

ADDITIONAL BIRDSONG RESOURCES

The birds themselves are an excellent resource, and the best practice for learning how to recognize the songs of a species is to listen to several individuals. Listen to how an individual varies his songs. Then listen to other individuals. The longer the session for each bird the better. You can also find someone who already knows birdsong to take you out *birding*.

For long listening sessions from individual birds, try the free websites for these two books:

Birdsong for the Curious Naturalist (www.BirdsongForTheCurious.com)
Listening to a Continent Sing (ListeningToAContinentSing.com)

The Cornell Laboratory of Ornithology (www.birds.cornell.edu/home) offers a lot of help. In their "All About Birds" (www.allaboutbirds.org/news/#), you can choose to listen to short recordings of anything you like. Their Merlin Bird ID app is a fun program for smartphones that helps to identify the common songs you are hearing. For more advanced fun, you could try their downloadable RavenLite software (ravensoundsoftware.com), which enables you to view birdsong spectrograms as you listen.

These two birdsong guides offer more listening opportunities for seventy-five eastern species and seventy-five western species:

The Backyard Birdsong Guide: Eastern and Central North America, Donald Kroodsma (Princeton University Press)
The Backyard Birdsong Guide: Western North America, Donald Kroodsma (Princeton University Press)

AUTHOR BIOS

© Janet Grenzke

© Erik Escoffier

© Xin Xin Sun

Donald Kroodsma is a world-renowned authority on birdsong and professor emeritus of ornithology at UMass Amherst. As a research scientist, he published widely on birdsong for more than fifty years. He has authored several books that introduce the general public to birdsong, including the award-winning *The Singing Life of Birds, The Backyard Birdsong Guides*, and, most recently, *Birdsong for the Curious Naturalist*. He lives in Massachusetts.

Léna Mazilu is an illustrator and designer. She is passionate about birds, nature, and education. Her first augmented reality children's book, *Chouette!*, has been translated into ten languages. With the assistance of an EU grant, she has since created the Birdie Memory app with Yoann Guény for the picture books *Ecoute les oiseaux* and *Listen to the Birds*. She lives in the countryside in Brittany, France, with her family.

Yoann Guény is an interactive developer from Paris. A graduate of the Gobelins School, he now specializes in online experiences and augmented reality.